FOOTBALL

Jean-Philippe Toussaint is the author of nine novels, all published by Éditions de Minuit in France, and the winner of numerous literary prizes, including the Prix Médicis for *Running Away* and the Prix Décembre for *The Truth about Marie*.

Shaun Whiteside is a translator from French, German, Italian and Dutch. His translations from French include novels by Amélie Nothomb, Patrick Rambaud, Michèle Desbordes, Georges-Marc Benamou, and Georges Simenon, as well as works of non-fiction by Pierre Bourdieu and Anne Sinclair. He lives in London.

'For any serious French writer who has come of age during the last thirty years, one question imposes itself above all others: what do you do after the nouveau roman? ... Foremost among this group, and bearing that quintessentially French distinction of being Belgian, is Jean-Philippe Toussaint... Toussaint's writing is remarkable for its conciseness, its elision.'
—— Tom McCarthy, author of *Satin Island*

'Toussaint is carving out one of the most fascinating literary oeuvres of our times.'
—— Nicholas Lezard, *Guardian*

'That there is nothing like this being written in English at the moment should be recommendation enough to the curious reader.'
—— Jonathan Gibbs, *Independent*

'Toussaint's prose is a pleasure to read: precise and increasingly muscular. There is a mesmerizing quality to his attention to detail... that marks him out as a successor to those other Minuit authors, the practitioners of the nouveau roman. But his is also a distinctive and original voice in French fiction.'
—— Adrian Tahourdin, *Times Literary Supplement*

'Toussaint has established himself as one of contemporary French literature's most distinctive voices, turning the existential tradition into something lighter, warmer and ultimately more open.'
—— Juliet Jacques, *New Statesman*

Fitzcarraldo Editions

FOOTBALL

JEAN-PHILIPPE TOUSSAINT

Followed by

ZIDANE'S MELANCHOLY

Translated by

SHAUN WHITESIDE

This is a book that no one will like, not intellectuals, who aren't interested in football, or football-lovers, who will find it too intellectual. But I had to write it, I didn't want to break the fine thread that still connects me to the world.

This story begins in 1998, with this date that suddenly strikes me as far away, sunk in the past, already buried heavily away in the finished twentieth century, which will seem to future generations as if it's from another era. It's an eminently strange number, this 1998, with this 1 and this 9 already looking so outmoded to our contemporary eyes, as if this date, 1998, though so close to us, though still so intimately connected to our lives, to our time, to our flesh and to our history, to our kisses and our sorrows, had accidentally sunk its teeth into the edge of the previous century and, inadvertently, found its feet dangling in the past. It's not our fault, but we are *compromised* by this past which we would have preferred to avoid. We know instinctively that the past, when we discover it in old photographs or archive pictures, always has a slightly awkward aspect to it, stiff, touching, even laughable, while the present – which is in fact merely its exact anticipation – is by contrast serious, reliable and worthy of respect. But it is in 1998 that this story begins, Jean, my son, was nine years old, Anna, my daughter, four. It was in 1998, very precisely on 10 June 1998 that, for the first time in my life, I went to a stadium to see a World Cup football match. The dates of the World Cups that followed – 2002, 2006, 2010, 2014 – are dates that might be called synonyms for 1998, but they are by no means homonyms, because they escape the withering of those strange and antiquated numbers, the 1 and 9 that mark them with a red light, like the lily on the shoulder of Milady de Winter, and inscribe them irrevocably in the past. Yes, 1998 is an old-fashioned date, a date that has aged badly, a date that had almost 'expired in its own lifetime', to repeat an expression I used in one of my novels, a date 'patinated by time, as if from the outset it bore within itself, like a corrosive poison hidden inside, the seed of its own dissolution, its definitive disappearance in the vast rush of time'.

Wonder

Football, like painting according to Leonardo da Vinci, is a *cosa mentale*; it is in the imagination that it is measured and appreciated. The nature of the wonder that football provokes derives from the fantasies of triumph and omnipotence that it generates in our minds. With my eyes closed, whatever my age and my physical condition, I am the star striker who scores the winning goal or the goalkeeper who throws himself in slow motion into the ether to make a crucial save. As a child I scored stunning goals (in my mind's eye, admittedly). The arms that I then raised to the sky in my parents' deserted sitting-room were as much a part of the ritual and the celebration as the goal that I had just scored. It was the celebrations, the congratulations, the kneeling on the pitch, the team mates throwing themselves on me and surrounding me, hugging me, showering me with praise, that I savoured most, not the move itself, it was my narcissistic triumph that brought me delight, not at all the possibility that it might one day happen in reality, that I might one day be able to control the ball marvellously well with my foot so that, with composure, with mastery, with skill, in a real stadium, facing real opponents, on a real pitch, I might propel it with a very pure twenty-five metre strike into the top corner of the opposing team's goal, in spite of the hopelessly floundering goalkeeper's desperate attempt to parry. The image is seductive, certainly, but I have other ambitions in life than being skilful with my feet. In my case it's more my hand, not only in art. Reality is almost always disappointing, that won't have escaped you. At the age of thirteen it was over, my footballing career was at an end. My last dreams of glory date from the spring of 1970, it was in Brussels, in the flat on rue Jules-Lejeune. My parents had just informed me that we were going to move to Paris, and I looked sadly at the door frame that separated the dining room from the sitting room and which acted as my imaginary goal, the setting for my last scenarios of footballing glory. An era was coming to an end. Reality for me now was this unknown future in Paris, the start of school in 1970 when I would join the fourth year as a boarder at a secondary school in Maisons-Laffitte. It would be a deracination, it would be the end of childhood, of happy days and of Brussels. My finest years would be over. Childhood is always followed by adolescence, and life, in reality, is uncompromising, the ball, while round, is recalcitrant and capricious, it resists us, thwarts us, humiliates us.

Stadiums

I never go to the stadium, there is no tradition of Dominical trips to the stadium in my family, my father never took me to see football matches, neither did my grandfathers, when I was knee high to a grasshopper I would have liked, with my little coat and my little cap, to go to the stadium with an adult who might have bought me a hot dog at half time. I have found a childhood photograph taken on the edge of the ponds of Ixelles, where I am with my grandfather, Juoazas

Lanskoronskis. You might have thought that we were about to go to the stadium at Anderlecht, or the one at Union Saint-Gilloise, but no, we weren't going to the stadium that day, and we didn't really look like supporters, we had more the look of writers on a jolly, he, my grandfather, who must have been the age I am now, with his austere look of a man of letters, and me with him, less than four years old, serious beside him like one of his venerable colleagues. It looks as if I was anticipating, by more than fifty years, the austere and taciturn appearance bestowed on writers, already prematurely bald, bald in my heart in some way, in solidarity with this Lithuanian grandfather, Colonel Lanskoronskis, who resembled Vladimir Nabokov physically and General Dourakine morally, and who also had a head made for hats, a roundabout way of saying he was bald. I have only been to the stadium in Brussels once, I had taken my son to a Belgium-Italy match during Euro 2000, and I have a few scattered memories of encounters at the Parc des Princes or the Stade de France, notably a Coupe de France final in 2002 between Lorient and Bastia, where we went as a family with some figatellu sausage and a Moor's head flag. In Corsica, I have a distant memory of going to a night-time match in Bastia with Charles Santandrea, my brother-in-law, it dates back to the early 1980s, I remember the floodlights in the old wooden stands of the Armand-Cesari Stadium. At the refreshment stand we bumped into Abbé Stra (look, it's Monsieur l'abbé!), who was wearing a little cross on the lapel of his jacket and an SC Bastia scarf around his neck. Abbé Stra – I would have been delighted to have invented this name, though I have only carefully collected it for a poss-ible future piece of writing – had been put in charge of our wedding preparations. But that's another story, the preparation for my wedding to Madeleine, in a hotel in Calacuccia, the Niolu, where, at the end of the meal, assuming a serious expression, Abbé Stra had said, 'Can I ask you an indiscreet question?' Madeleine and I, we must have been on the cheese course, let's say between figs and cheese, had modestly lowered our eyes to our plates, silently nodded (I could see that Madeleine was exploding with laughter inside), and asked us, in a cautious voice: 'Have you known each other for a long time?' If I had been feeling witty I could have answered, with Gide: 'There are no indiscreet questions, only answers sometimes are.' But I merely told him the truth, that we had known each other for two years. But I'm wandering off, I'm dawdling and shilly-shallying, without ever losing sight of my central idea, don't worry. No, this is what I was getting at: when I'm at home, in the cities I live in, in Brussels or in Corsica, I never go to stadiums. Otherwise I'd have been at Heysel in 1985 and Furiani in 1992.

Jerseys

I like that moment, going to the stadium, when, climbing the concrete stairs of the stands inside among the crowd of spectators to get to my seat, I emerge into the open air of the terraces and down below I see the *absolute* green of the pitch beneath the powerful floodlights of the stadium. I no longer have the eyes of a child, but I still see the magic of colours at football with the naive innocence of childhood, the age-old green of the turf and the jerseys of the players, the timeless colours of the national teams, the blue of France or Italy, the red of Spain, the orange of the Netherlands, not to mention the striped sky-blue and white of Argentina. Everything returns to a state of order, nature becomes immutable and reassuring again when I see, as I did at the final in Yokohama in 2002, the Germans playing in black shorts and white jerseys against the Brazilians in yellow and green, but it is with a little twinge of annoyance in my heart, of aesthetic dissatisfaction and metaphysical unease, that I see Brazil playing in dark blue or, even worse, the German players afflicted with that laterally striped red and black rugby jersey (is it Toulouse, is it Toulon?) that they wore for the semi-final of the 2014 World Cup in Brazil. I feel wronged, not myself (I've seen worse), but the child I used to be, who is deprived of the simple and reassuring happiness of seeing for all eternity the Germans moving in black shorts and white jerseys on football grounds.

Childhood

In Brussels, in the playground of primary school no. 9, we used to play football at break time and the criterion used to separate the two teams was not little versus big or fair versus dark or year four versus year five, it was Moral versus Religion. At the start of the year, in this secular school on rue Américaine in Ixelles, you effectively had to choose between Moral and Religion, according to whether or not our parents or we ourselves wanted to take catechism classes. While Religion were initiated into the edifying episodes of the life of Christ and the reading of the Bible, the rest had a kind of rudimentary civic education which had been given, and I only grasped the whole flavour of it years later, the word Moral. Still, at break, we pupils, grabbing hold of this divisive criterion which seemed to us to have biblical simplicity and which had the further advantage of being perfectly trans-generational (as many believers as non-believers among the little ones as the big ones, among potential defenders and putative attackers), in the playground in rue Américaine, we played Moral versus Religion football matches – and Religion, of which I was one (I was always very Religion, at least until year six), were devils with the ball.

Avenue Louise

I'm in Brussels, it's an old picture, perhaps on avenue Louise, I'm with a few friends, we're in year six Latin-Maths at Athénée Robert Catteau, there's Thierry Degulne, Dominique Deredde, Philippe Warneck, perhaps Alain van Vinck, perhaps Éric Peeters, and we're standing with our satchels in front of the window of an electronic goods shop, mocking, with our juvenile insolence and our schoolboy irony, the first colour televisions showing the games of the 1970 World Cup. We don't yet have a colour television at home, and we laugh at the sight of the football players on screen getting ahead of their jerseys, as if the player running on the pitch, by virtue of their speed and the intensity of their dribbling, had managed to leave his physical envelope behind and now pursued his moves in black and white, leaving behind him the colour of his jersey, which followed him only after a slight delay. It made us laugh in front of the shop window, this new technology which hadn't quite been perfected. Even if there was an undeniable poetic dimension to it, the way the players left in their wake like a halo of themselves in a kind of slow-motion stretch of the colour of their jerseys. Recently, at the Grand Palais in Paris, I saw a video by Bill Viola, which plays with that switch between black and white and colour, with three women passing in a single image from snowy, blurry black and white, through an invisible boundary, a virtual curtain, a kind of symbolic checkpoint, as if moving between existence and non-being, birth and death.

Seasons

As I grow older, I realise that football is connected with the seasons, or rather that there is a football season, a happy time of year, like the strawberry season or the cherry season (always in June and July where the World Cup is concerned), which comes round every four years with the regularity of a leap-year seasonal fruit. Each time it was the wait, the incipient curiosity, the interest, remote at first, that we take in qualifying matches, then the first glances of the connoisseur when the date of the final tournament is established, eyes glistening at the sight of the first mouth-watering big games. Sometimes the preparation begins upstream, as it did for the 2002 World Cup, for which I prepared my trip to Japan six months in advance, bought tickets on the internet for the stadiums, booked hotels in Tokyo, in Kyoto, in Kobe, drew up a programme of readings and talks at different universities, and established the principle of a collaboration with newspapers and a Japanese literary magazine. Then, inevitably, the time comes for the first match. In 2002, I had landed in Tokyo just a few hours earlier, and even before I'd unpacked my suitcase

I was already watching the opening match on television in my hotel room in Shinjuku. Then, throughout the tournament, football rocks us hour by hour, it gives a rhythm to our life, it scans it, marks it out, punctuates it, accompanies it from a distance, like a summer sun whose presence one no longer notices, so regular are the benefits that it brings us, so constant the meetings that it arranges for us. There are matches every day, at the end of the afternoon, in the evening, at night. Towards the end of the tournament, the games are more spaced out, imperceptibly, to stir up our expectations and heighten our appetites. When the dénouement comes, football transports us even further, it ignites us. I have jumped with joy all alone in deserted living-rooms. During penalty shoot-outs, I have prayed mentally, I have held my breath, fingers crossed, eyes closed, open, hoping, pleading, fiddling with my grigris, clutching my talismans, imploring St Anthony of Padua, plunging mental needles into the opponents' calves. To these seasonal invariants, which come back with the reassuring regularity of tides or heavenly cycles – football as natural phenomenon or universal invariant – the question being not knowing whether there will be a next episode, but whether the vintage will be good (if it will be a *grand cru* or a bad year, like 2010, a *grand millésime* for Bordeaux and bitter plonk for French football), some adjustable variables are added, like the list of qualifying countries or the location of the competition, which has no constant base but moves around the world with the majestic slowness of a cargo criss-crossing the world, from Asia to Europe (Seoul, Tokyo, Berlin), stopping off in Africa and crossing the Atlantic towards South America (Johannesburg, Rio de Janeiro) with its cortège of players and officials, its caravan of trainers and physios, of journalists and media, peregrinating from continent to continent.

The Trophy

The World Cup trophy is an object made of gold, short and stocky, a bit more than thirty centimetres tall, which seems to end in a ball or a stylised image of the globe. Apparently it represents two athletes placed in a transcendent state by victory, lifting the Earth, and not, as I thought at first sight, the curve of a glans emerging from a drawn-back foreskin (although we may agree that it remains indisputably phallic). Since the original vanished after being stolen in Brazil in 1983, the trophy now travels by plane under strict guard. It is a curious fate for this contemporary totem, this universal fetish and much-coveted object *par excellence*, protected in safes and transported in armed coffers under the watch of policemen wearing Kevlar jackets and armed with machine-guns, which is finally removed from its case on the day of the final so that it can be held aloft, and kissed, in mondovision, by the captains of the winning World Cup teams, by Didier Deschamps at the Stade de France in 1998, then by Cafu in 2002 at Yokohama stadium, then by I can't remember who in Berlin (my memory, like certain illnesses, sometimes has diplomatic lacunae) then by the players of the winning team who trot in a cluster, socks lowered, a national flag draped like a shawl around their shoulders, preceded by a swarm of press photographers wearing apple-green chasubles taking pictures of them with telephoto lenses while running backwards, as the players pass the trophy from hand to hand and lift it towards the stands of Yokohoma stadium or the Olympiastadion in Berlin, where I am too, standing in the terraces, one amongst eighty thousand cheering the players on in this jubilant crowd.

Chauvinism

Football allows you to be, not nationalist, which would have a detestable political connotation that leaves me entirely cold, and not even patriotic, but *chauvinistic*, by which I mean a non-duped, second-level nationalism, an *ironic nationalism*, the oxymoron is perfect, there are no terms that are more antinomian, the charm of the adjective seems to contradict everything displeasing that the word might have, a childish nationalism, of the order of a simple-minded boast, a euphoric, playful fanfare: long live Belgium! A nationalism brandishing caps rather than concepts, charms rather than values, and spreading around the terraces of the stadiums to the sound of whistles, maracas and foghorns. During a match I am in a state of simple-minded comfort, the more flavoursome for being accompanied by a temporarily acceptable intellectual regression. I become biased, aggressive, vehement, combative, I insult the referee, I curse and castigate him. I vilify the other team. I give free rein to the impulses of violence and aggression that normally have no place in my personality. I agree to stupidity and ordinariness. I award myself a treat – let's call it a catharsis.

The last time I filled in a visa application form for the People's Republic of China, I hesitated before filling in the section 'current profession', which provided about fifteen possibilities including businessman, artist, crew member, member of parliament, member of the armed forces, farmer, cleric or aid worker. There was no box for 'writer', so I ticked the one for 'artist'. Arriving at the Chinese visa centre on rue Neerveld in Brussels, I handed my file to the lady at the counter, who was perfectly bilingual (Chinese-Dutch), but didn't speak French. English, for better or for worse, would be our common language. She set aside the copy of my plane ticket and my hotel room reservation and carefully reread the answers I had given on the form, with a high-lighter in her hand which she kept a certain distance above the sheet of paper, vaguely threatening, like certain drug-sniffer dogs that you see in airport halls which make you feel uneasy even if you have nothing to be guilty about. She stopped abruptly, highlighter in the air, frowning. What is your job? she said to me. Writer, I said. But why did you claim you were an artist? she said indignantly. She seemed outraged. How to answer that one? I thought for a moment. Try and explain to her that in a sense one might consider writers to be artists. No, that would have involved us in excessively long, potentially sulphurous and provocative, semantic and casuistical debates. Then, being impertinent and arro-gantly replying that it wasn't just football players who were artists these days. Even less: without taking her eyes off me, she would probably have pressed a button with the toe of her shoe to call security, and goodbye to my trip to China. No, I stayed calm and asked her politely which box, in her view, I should have ticked. As if it was perfectly obvious, she indicated the last one: other (please specify). That was my current profession: other (please specify), and she prodded the correct box with her finger. She took a pen and furiously crossed out the 'artist' line that I had ticked, as if to erase the trace of the insane pretention that had gripped me of taking myself for an artist, and invited me to stick to what I really was: a writer, nothing more.

Open Reduction

It's often childhood that rises to the surface when I think about football. We're in 1969, I'm eleven years old, it's afternoon, I have no idea what season it is, autumn or early spring, and I'm playing football at the Renier-Chalon playground in Brussels, on a piece of waste ground which served as a football pitch, enough for our dreams of glory. My friends at the time are called Thierry Deguine, Philippe Warneck, I don't know if they're with me that day, I don't think so, and I'm playing, I'm giving it my all, I'm running, I'm sweating a lot, I have a curl on my forehead that's falling into my eyes. I have no idea what I'm wearing that day, I'm certainly not in sports gear, tracksuits aren't yet fashionable in the late 1960s, so I must be wearing long trousers and a woollen jumper knitted by my grandmother with the sleeves rolled up. There are a few boys my age, and I'm among them, in this human cloud that runs in a clump after the ball amidst a halo of dust that reaches me across time even today. I'm at the heart of that undifferentiated cloud and I see the scene in slow motion, almost fifty years on, stretching and dilating, another, older boy runs beside me and catches up with me, there's a brief shoulder-to-shoulder contact, or else he pushes me aside deliberately with his arm, and I fall, the image is slow, ethereal, infinitely dispersed in the halo of memory, I fall sideways, forearm first, violently to the ground. I'm on the floor, I'm stunned. I struggle to my feet, my arm looks odd, it's soft, round, disjointed. I take a few steps, no one's paying me any attention, and I walk away, my arm swollen, dissociated from my body, drawing a circle beside me. I leave the pitch, holding back my tears, or maybe I'm crying, I'm eleven years old and I'm crying in the street as I go home, I hurry up outside the garage on rue Léon-Jouret, the door of the workshop is wide open and letting a hot smell of engine oil escape into the district, the contents of which I imagine I can smell across time. I go into the sitting-room on rue Jules-Lejeune, my mother is reading on a sofa, she lifts her head without looking at me and tells me to stop snivelling. I walk over to her and she spots my arm, she understands the gravity of the situation and calls my father on the phone to ask him to join us. We take a taxi to the hospital, I'm between my father and my mother, each time the taxi goes over a bump I'm in pain, but I try to be brave, I grit my teeth, I'm not crying any more. At the hospital there are hours of waiting, I'm given an x-ray. The doctor, in white overalls, his face grim, comes back towards my parents with the x-rays and tells them he's going to try to avoid an 'open reduction'. My father is struck by the expression, I know he will remember it for a long time. It's understandable, it must be a little alarming to hear a doctor telling you he might have to carry out an open reduction on your eleven-year-old son's arm, but those are the words he used, open reduction, *réduction sanglante*, it must be the

22

precise medical term, when the fracture is displaced and the arm must be opened to put the bones back in place. In the end the operation won't be necessary, my fracture – double fracture of the left arm, radius and cubitus – will be resorbed with a plaster. There you are, football is that too, in reality: my tears as a little boy and the ground of a piece of waste land that has the roughness of the real.

Football Time

The interest you take in a football match essentially has a very particular relationship with time, a relationship of precise appropriateness, of perfect simultaneity between the unfolding match and the passing of time. Football cannot bear the slightest gap, the tiniest disjunction, and it is precisely because football merges so perfectly with the course of time, because it so fully embraces its passing, because it inhabits it so closely, that while we are watching football it brings us a kind of metaphysical wellbeing that diverts us from our miseries and takes us away from the thought of death. While we watch a football match, during the very particular time that passes while we are at the stadium or in front of our television, we move in an abstract and reassuring world, we are, for the duration of the game, in a cocoon of time, preserved from the wounds of the outside world, away from the contingencies of reality, of its pains and its dissatisfactions, in which real time, the irremediable time that drags us constantly towards death, seems numbed and as if anaesthetised. It is also the reason why football, in the moment when we are watching it, develops such a suspenseful quality. When we watch a football match, the future, in the short term, is unresolved, it is fundamentally open. The future unveils itself before our eyes, we discover it, piecemeal, in real time. At the precise moment when we are watching a football match, the result is unknown and the outcome uncertain, so it is impossible to let our attention wander for a moment, to leave our seat (or at our own risk, because it is at that precise moment – at any moment – that a goal may be scored). That's why a football match immediately ceases to be interesting as soon as we know the final result. As soon as the invisible thread connecting football to the passage of time is broken, as soon as it is stripped of its dimension of irreversibility, its grace and brilliance immediately vanish: nothing remains but the materiality of the players, the emergence of the prosaic and the violence of the real, the sweat, the shouts, the blows, the absurd unreality of twenty guys running after a ball on a pitch.

Perishable Goods

All in all, football is a perishable product, its use-by date is immediate. It must be consumed straight away, like oysters, whelks, langoustines, prawns (I will spare you the exhaustive composition of the *plateau*). It must be enjoyed fresh, in the intensity of the moment, in the heat of immediacy. Football does not age well, it is a diamond that only shines brightly today. We never watch repeats of old football matches on television. Even legendary finals are faded, their perfume has vanished into the dust of time, they remain far behind us and become a familiar component of our past, it is only in our memories that they may still quiver with ephemeral grace. Then, over time, football changes its dimension. From the perishable product that it was, it becomes timeless and attains the status of a myth or legend. In the long term, in our minds, it is then replaced by the extract, the quotation, the spark or the fragment. It will not occur to us to watch the whole of the 1966 Wembley World Cup Final, but we will search the internet for Geoff Hurst's disputed goal to examine it carefully on our computer. It's the same with cycling. Who today would want to see in its entirety the broadcast of a long stage of the Tour de France, however legendary, like the famous duel between Poulidor and Anquetil in the ascent of the Puy-de-Dôme in 1964? Even if we could access all those images we wouldn't want to, we need an open space, one not saturated with information, which leaves an active space for our imagination. Nothing, when it comes to dreaming and fleetingly finding the essence of the past, can match a single image, rare, precious, iconic, like that photograph, its colours slightly faded, of Eddy Merckx on the cover of an old cycling magazine kept under plastic film spotted by chance on a second-hand book-dealer's stall, with the yellow jersey of the Tour de France or the touching Havana-brown jersey of the Molteni team, which suddenly reactivates the past with greater certainty than we might get from the proliferation of pointless details of a fastidious television broadcast.

Writing

Words, perhaps, have the power to reactivate the magic of football, not the words of the press articles which will relate the episodes of the previous day's match, texts that go out of fashion as quickly as the matches they describe, but words of poetry, or literature, which come to brush against football, grasp its movement, caress its colours, stroke its charms, flatter its enchantments, taking football as a motif, talking about its fluidity and the elasticity of the ebb and flow of the offensive and defensive waves which we observe from above, from the overhanging stands. Some of the texts I have devoted to football were written more than ten years ago. In them I have tackled only accessory, insignificant or minor subjects, which I have compared to the unmoveable pillars of time and melancholy. I have always stayed away from the great theoretical debates concerning football as a social or political phenomenon. I'm not interested in football as a symbol of globalisation or a metaphor for society. From a strategic point of view, football strikes me as entirely summary, almost simplistic, the respective advantages of the different systems of play (4-2-4, 4-4-2 or the *catenaccio*) are of elementary simplicity compared to the skilful subtleties of the smallest line of play in chess, and the horrible word *coaching*, which blends awkwardness with disproportion, is a big word for not very much: the appropriateness of substitutions and choosing the opportune moment to make them. But here we suddenly move from the seriousness of the childhood universe to the childishness of the world of adults. The football of adults leaves me cold. As a citizen I am happy to raise a worried eyebrow over violence in the stadiums, racism, homophobia and hooliganism, I am happy to be shocked by the sums paid for transfers and the exorbitant salaries of the players, but I will not devote more than a parenthesis to them (oof, tired already – end of parenthesis).

That may be what's secretly at stake in these lines, trying to transform football, its vulgar, coarse and perishable matter, into an immovable form bound up with the seasons, with melancholy, time and childhood. Never have I, as I did in Japan in 2002, sensed such a perfect concordance of times, in which the time of football, re-assuring and abstract had, for a month, not substituted but slid, merged into the most enormous gangue of real time, and had made me feel the passing of time like a long protective caress, beneficial, tutelary, apotropaic. Nothing can happen to us while we are watching a football match: as in the advantageous frontal proximity of a woman's sexual parts in certain positions of the act of love, which instantly disperses the dread of death, which anaesthetises it and melts it away into the moisture and sweetness of the embrace, football, while we are watching it, holds us radically at a distance from death. I am pretending to write about football, but I am writing, as always, about the passing of time.

FRANCE, 1998

I can't dissociate football from dreams and childhood.

I am now a little over forty years old, I wrote in the first piece I devoted to football on the occasion of the 1998 World Cup, I have a certain *je ne sais quoi* of Bobby Charlton, a hint of Lord-Chandos-style sceptical melancholy in my facial expression, the physical fitness of Maradona, and I'm as clumsy with a ball at my feet as, let's say, Dugarry, and I don't know if it's because I'm starting to get older, if it's childhood and dreams that are fading, but I'm starting to get a bit fed up with football. I prefer poetry (I'm barely joking).

Even as regards my timeless enthusiasm for the Belgian team, impeccable until now, I'm starting to wonder if it too isn't idealised, not to say solipsistic, virtual and abstract. Because, thinking about it properly:

1) I no longer know anyone in the Belgian team that's going to play the World Cup in France in 1998. Apart from Wilmots, of course (but everyone knows Wilmots).

2) I don't even know who the coach is any more. Once, at least, it was van Himst! it was van Moer! and those glorious names that I was brought up with still sound like as many Flemish, metallic madeleines to my melancholy ears.

3) Deep down I don't really like the Belgian team's jersey. And, at the risk of casting one last shadow over the staunch loyalty of my approximate chauvinism, I don't really like their style of play.

A style of play that is, no doubt, solid, athletic
and collective, in what we might call at best the
German style, with guys like Gerets or Philippe
Albert and which, in the worst of cases, evoke the
style of play of teams like Waregem or Beveren,
with selflessly dedicated lads, their socks caked
with mud, in the Patrick Revelli-mould. Eleven
Patrick Revellis, that's the team! A nightmare!

And yet it was for these shoulders of mutton
That I have rhymed!
I would happily break your hips
For having loved!

KOREA/JAPAN, 2002

All through June 2002, when I went to Japan to follow the football World Cup, I had a feeling that football and Japan, even though they are contradictory – tumult and tranquillity, fire and water – were merging together to give birth to a new element, an unknown and delicious alliance that as yet had no name. As the days passed, slow and inexorable, gentle and fluid, and I followed the football matches in the stadiums or on television, the Kamo River flowed in Kyoto to the peaceful and regular rhythm of the passing of time, day and night, sometimes under a very clear sky, with a dazzling sun that lit the banks of close-cropped grass all the way to Sanjo Bridge, sometimes under a fine rain that dripped sadly from the ribs of my transparent umbrella, with a motionless ash-coloured crane standing in my field of vision. I remember those nights by the river and the stone path that crosses the ford in a constant lapping of water, and the four seasons of that mild year of 2002 pass constantly in my memory, all seasons at once, following one another in sequence during those June days in Japan. Straight away there was the high summer of the first matches in Kobe, which were played in the furnace of summer afternoons, in which the burning heat of 3 p.m. reminded my fragile skin and my narrowed eyes of the sun of Corsica or Tunisia, then there was the delicious spring evening of the same Kobe stadium some weeks later, on the evening of the wonderful Brazil-Belgium match when, in front of my eyes, the eyes of a marvelling child, a sea breeze gently rippled the flags of the corner posts in the tepid night, then at last it was autumn, or perhaps it was already winter, the deluge and desolation of the sad, big stadium of Sendai on the day when Japan was eliminated. This unique sensation, made of past time, of sparse images, of scattered Japanese tastes and smells – the very matter, immaterial, of memory – I would like to try and restore everything indecipherable and incoherent about it. I would like not to part the things that still fit closely together in my mind as memories of that month of June 2002, not artificially separate football and Japan, but restore them as I experienced them, all together, in trains and stadiums, amongst the crowd of blue-jerseyed supporters, in that humid June heat that sticks clothes to the body or under stubborn rain that wet my face in dribs and drabs in the sultry ambiance of a foggy Tokyo.

I arrived in Japan a few hours before the kick-off of the 2002 World Cup. Tokyo hadn't changed very much since my last visit, I just noticed through the porthole of the plane that had just landed in Narita a big inscription traced on the ground in letters of multi-coloured flowers pecked at by birds: 2002 FIFA WORLD CUP. Our Boeing 757, still coated with a fine dew of droplets of condensation, sent the little birds flying as it passed. Already, as tiny heralds of the sporting event, still virtual and invisible, which I was going to witness, I had noticed when boarding the plane in Roissy the unfamiliar presence on a Paris-Tokyo flight of several Irishmen on the plane, with discreet scarves peeping out from under their jackets, or a big pitch-green jersey, Stade de France turf or Yokohama green, probably going to Niigata, via Tokyo, for Ireland-Cameroon on 1 June. So they would be my first supporters, the first I would encounter during this seventeenth edition of the football World Cup. Four years ago, in Paris, it was the Scots, much more hardcore in their woollen kilts, their square shoulders and their royal blue jerseys, packed around me like salmon, singing at the tops of their voices in the crammed metro carriage taking us to the Stade de France for the opening match of the previous edition (Brazil-Scotland: 2-1).

It was greyish in Tokyo the morning I arrived, hot, heavy, foggy. My mind numb, I fought against sleep in the big, almost empty orange 'Airport Limousine' coach that took us into the city in the early morning, snoozing on my seat together with the few Japanese present in the bus, a people quick to take a little public nap in shared transport (you would think that the whole nation suffered from chronic jet lag). In short, Tokyo wore its usual face in those first days of the World Cup. The most I can say is that I was woken up in my hotel room at about four o'clock in the morning by a confused urban racket that mixed with my dreams and finished in disarray with a chorus of male voices chanting incomprehensible pleasantries, invariably punctuated by ENGLAND! ENGLAND! while, through the half-open curtains of the room there passed a dawning day, still milky with the air of Helsinki daybreaks. It's the first time too that, in a Tokyo hotel, a fellow guest has asked me at reception which country I came from, and who, when I told him I was from Belgium, asked me when I was playing. When I was playing? But I was still as plain-clothes as possible, dark trousers and black jacket, no tricorn or scarf, hunting horn, devil jersey or red BELGIUM cap, but, with a lot of self-control, working out what he was referring to, I told him I was playing tomorrow, tomorrow night. Good luck, he said.

During those first few days in Tokyo, I stayed in a small hotel in Shibuya, at the end of a street of love hotels lit by multi-coloured neon signs, which rose at a slight gradient no distance from Bunkamura. Since arriving, I divided my time between lectures at universities and match broadcasts on television. I took my meals at restaurants with Japanese professors who welcomed me into their classes, or alone in my hotel room, snacking in front of England-Sweden or Spain-Paraguay on television, sitting on my bed in my cramped little room, my food cartons spread out around me on the bed covers, the plastic film that covered the dishes already rolled up in a ball in the bin, the chopsticks separated, opening the sachet of soy to pour it carefully over the food, fingers slightly sticky with sauce. I like picnicking like that in hotel bedrooms when I'm in Japan, it's a pleasure to leave the hotel to go and dig out some local convenience store, 7-Eleven or FamilyMart, open twenty-four hours a day, and assemble a menu among the shelves by carefully choosing different dishes from the refrigerated compartments (sushi here, seaweed there, fragments of pumpkin, aubergines, spinach), then to head towards the drinks and hesitate between the different kinds of tea, before opening the door of a freezer to take out, for dessert, a little tub of green tea ice-cream (in Kobe, after the Brazil-Belgium match that ended at night, I wasn't the only one doing this kind of shopping before going back to the hotel, there was a real procession of customers who passed through the Lawson store before filing back to their rooms through the luxurious hotel lobby, clutching plastic bags).

The first match I had a ticket for during the World Cup jointly organized by Korea and Japan was

Japan-Belgium on 4 June 2002 in Saitama, it was Japan's opening match, the co-organiser's entry into the fray, the match of a whole nation (Japan-Belgium, poor us!). A rumour was already circulating that to get to the stadium it would be wise to allow a journey time of three to four hours, there would be at least sixty thousand Japanese spectators, and apparently I had no idea about Japanese crowds given that two or three hundred thousand people will sometimes hurry to see a firework display around a tiny stretch of water. So I prudently left the hotel early in the afternoon, carrying a light rucksack containing my binoculars, a camera and my supporter's cap. Tens of kilometres away from the stadium, before I even entered the metro, I started to notice the first blue jerseys in the streets of Tokyo, those blue Japanese jerseys like the ones worn by the French team, most bearing the 7 of Nakata or the 5 of Inamoto, the 8 of Ono or the 10 of Nakayama, and, all these blue jerseys, like isolated droplets which, resembling one another, finally form a thin stream flowing in the streets, then a great watercourse, a blue river, increasingly swollen, leaving the mouths of the metro and spreading along the avenues to enter the stadium where, suddenly, huge waves form and surge along the crowded stands, and where, amidst an enormous hub-bub, rises the irrepressible blue tide of sixty thousand Japanese supporters on their feet, chanting the name of their country: NIPPON, NIPPON!

A few seconds before kick-off, in the electric atmosphere of the stands of the Saitama stadium, while the players were already in place and the match was about to begin, four amazing fighter planes suddenly flew over the stadium at a low altitude, brushing the rooftops and disappearing with a deepening roar and leaving in their wake unsettling scraps of smoke and sinister reminiscences of war, violence and air-raids. But apart from these childish militaristic displays, the evening was as gentle as could be. The whistle was blown, and when, like an unexpected deliverance, Belgium opened the scoring with a spectacular acrobatic scissor-kick by Wilmots, I leapt from my seat, arms in the air, turning in a circle and giddily jumping around in the stands, not knowing where to go, who to celebrate the event with, before spotting another Belgian as isolated as I was among the terraces. We gauchely hurried towards each other, not knowing how to concelebrate our goal, merely striking our palms violently together, like two American basketball players who have just pulled off some kind of feat. Nothing more, we didn't exchange a word, I don't even know if this man spoke French (it was one of the strangest relationships that I have ever had in my life), finding him again a quarter of an hour later in the same place to repeat the same gesture after Belgium's second goal. I could have settled for celebrating the Belgian goals, but I must confess that, almost without admitting it to myself, I always felt a secret satisfaction at the sight of this stadium exploding and trembling on its foundations each time the Japanese scored a goal. In the end, this draw suited me wonderfully well, it was even the exact score that I had wished for. I remember that, in early December, when the group stages were drawn, I had sent an email to Kan Nozaki, my Japanese translator, to tell him I hoped we would be outdoing each other with courtesies at this Japan-Belgium game and that, knowing by reputation the excellent manners of his countrymen, I hoped that the Japanese would have the exquisite politeness not to beat us, and that we would have the elegance not to take advantage of this to win.

*

Almost thirty degrees at all times since I arrived in Japan, heavy, humid weather over Tokyo, a uniformly blue sky in the Kansai, slightly windy, with, here and there, via a sliding door suddenly opening up on to Osaka Bay, a gust of sea air catching you in the face. Everywhere here, in the shops and the hotels, in the restaurants and in the trains, serene air conditioning units hum, spreading icy air in public spaces, so that if you die of heat in the stadiums you shiver in the trains that take you there. Curious, however, that the Japanese, who overheat their homes in winter as enthusiastically as they air-condition in the summer, prefer to have things too hot in winter and too cold in summer (while the opposite would save them billions of Yen). Kobe Stadium, in the middle of the afternoon, is a furnace. On the way back from games, standing in a freezing metro train, face damp and clothes sticking to your body, on which dusty sweat is drying, I need a good post-game shower as much as the players to recover. If there are enough gaps in my own diary and I am allowed a relatively large amount of recovery between games, I still find myself having to juggle geography and timetables, because I had a match that finished one evening in Tokyo, and another that began the following early afternoon in Kobe. But the Shinkansen has no secrets for me any more, any more than the Shinkaisoku, the Kaisoku and the Futsu, which bring you to Hyogo and Kobe Stadium.

If the revelation of the group stages is without a doubt the Japanese team, whose aerial, fluid and charming game inspires the crowds of punkettes in kimonos and girls in blue jerseys, the real surprise, it seems to me, is that Japan has lined up a team of little blonds. Where as their opponents in the same group, the Russians and the Belgians, look as if they've come straight out of the twentieth century, with their fuddy-duddy air of soldiers or athletes, short hair and sticking-out ears, with a lorry-driver's ear-ring in their earlobes (but never a piercing in their tongues), the Japanese have a team of stars, rock singers and juvenile leads, shining, according to the crazed curls on their youthful heads, with all the Venetian shades of blond and auburn, not to mention the bright orange Iroquois of Kazuyuki Toda, the Iron Mask, Jean-Paul Gaultier all the way, of Tsuneyasu Miyamoto, and the always strong shaven head of Shinji Ono, already a classic, that you also see on Roberto Carlos and Carsten Jancker, Pierluigi Collina and me, the good old billiard ball that could be said to come from a brilliant French tradition which includes both Barthez (the goalkeeper) and Foucault (the philosopher).

I've been back in Tokyo for several days, in Meguro, in the guest room of Meiji Gakuin University. It's a quiet area, wooded and residential, which reminds me a little of Kyoto, with narrow, sloping streets lined with little white houses. On the first day I woke up at about six in the morning and went out into the deserted alleyways, where a scorching sun was already shining, to have breakfast. I hesitated and prevaricated, before I was drawn to a sumptuous residence with the air of a museum, a temple or a manor-house. Behind the boundary wall, some vans with the hotel's coat of arms, abandoned in the car park. I advanced along

40

the edge of the park towards the main building, look-ing for the lobby where I hoped to find a newspaper in English, when I found myself face to face with a giant football jersey, in blue fabric, at least five metres high by three metres wide, with the FFF crest of the French Football Federation embroidered on the chest, erected in the car park between two metal posts that held it out, motionless in the peaceful morning. No breeze made the armpits quiver, and it looked crucified, that blue jersey, which, a few hours later, was going to be low-ered to half-mast because of the premature elimination of the French team from this seventeenth World Cup, while the players' hotel reservations would be cancelled, their suitcases returned, the presents and the flowers unordered. I turned on my heels, hailing this curious coincidence which had brought me by chance to the hotel that the French team would have occupied if it had pursued its course in Japan.

*

I encountered full stadiums and deserted cafés. I saw games in noodle bars with their walls covered with pleonastic pictures of the dishes you're eating and with, up in a corner, a small square television on a shelf, broadcasting the match of the day and bringing to mind a similar little television, snowy and blurred, in a café in Siena in Italy where I followed the World Cup final between Holland and Argentina in 1978. I followed, late in the evening, games in the hip cafés of Shibuya or Omote Sando, with bare, glowing red walls, where you're no longer quite sure if you're in a café or a contemporary art gallery, in front of a giant screen where footballers four metres high move, looking like ragged silhouettes by Bacon. The customers aren't sure where they are either, rather indifferent to the match, before some agonising cries in extra time drag them from their torpor and they crane their necks to look sceptically at the giant screen behind them. I saw a crucial match by the Japanese team in a crammed amphitheatre at Meiji Gakuin University, the tables and chairs lined up against the walls, students and teachers sitting cross-legged on the floor, or straddling the tables, standing against the wall and leaning on the doors, and I trembled along with the Japanese public, turning round to give enthusiastic high-fives to girls in order to welcome the goals of Morishima and Nakata, before taking the floor, at the end of the match, in a room that was more obedient and more studious, not as a writer, my first hat, or as a film-maker, my second, but as a lover of football (my third hat, the red cap with BELGIUM written on it in gold letters), with Professor G., who has published two knowledgeable books on football and is also a specialist in Valéry (for a long time I thought it was Proust). But what I had never done was listen to the commentary of a football match on Japanese radio. By some unfortunate quirk of fate, one of my lectures had been scheduled to start at exactly the same time as the Japan-Turkey second-round game, and as soon as the lecture was over, knowing that there were still a few minutes of play before the end of the match and possible extra time, accompanied by my hosts and a small group of students running down the stairs beside me, we crossed the deserted campus in search of a hypothetical television before making do in the French department, with a radio that several people were already gathered around, to follow the end of the game in their company. Arms crossed, serious and concentrating, I listened carefully to the commentary, despite the absence of a simultaneous translation that would have allowed me to understand what was happening on the pitch (without having made much progress, I've started to understand a few Japanese words, such as *corner*, *penalty* and *free kick*). My senses on the alert, I read with unease the expressions on the faces of the students, while my ears, pricked like a cat's, listened out for danger or promises of a goal, trying to interpret the variations in intensity of the commentator's voice, which went from a regular purr during the midfield phases of the game to a rapid crescendo at the approach of goals by the opposing team, to the brief fit of hysteria, close to apoplexy, to the moment of the cross and the generally failed attempt at a volley.

For several days I don't encounter any more football jerseys in the streets. It's down time, the days for taking a break and recovering before the last games. I haven't got stadium tickets before the semi-final in Saitama and the final in Yokohama, and, to compound matters, I'm in Kyoto, which has never been very keen on football. Even the Pig and Whistle, the celebrated English pub on the edge of Sanjo, seems to have adopted the city's reserve its own, and by the entrance there hangs a long list of prohibitions meant for potential supporters, some full of common sense ('Entry will be refused if the bar is full'), the last more surprising for a bar showing football ('Entry will be refused to persons wearing football team shirts'). But it's Kyoto, and it's the summer. I listen to the vague sounds of water that can be heard in the distance. What does football matter, in the end? Time passes, and, on the bridges, fleeting female silhouettes on bicycles, umbrellas in their hands.

Now that the rainy season has really begun (until now it had this special feature, for a rainy season, that it didn't rain – and the Japanese, without blinking an eye, then call it a *dry* rainy season), there's nothing better to do in a foggy Tokyo where a fine drizzle like atomised water falls constantly, than to go and take shelter in football stadiums, which are covered from nightfall. By chance conversations and encounters, I made the acquaintance in Tokyo of a Frenchman who works for a Japanese television channel and, by virtue of arriving at the stadium a few hours early and making some secret-agent manoeuvres – a quick call from a public phone-box to a mobile phone by the entrance to the stadium to announce my arrival, exchange of badges and security checks – I was able to follow the Brazil-Turkey semi-final from the press box. At first I even squatted a little commentator's cabin, with a personalised control display in front of each seat (I was inches away from putting the headphones on and commentating live on the match for some unknown television channel, just to look more credible), before I was dislodged by some amiable lady from the organisation who asked me to move up a row, to what are so prettily known as the observers' seats.

After more than an hour of observation in the deserted Saitama stadium, which was filling up in dribs and drabs, the Turkish players came to scout out the ground. They weren't yet wearing their kit, flip-flops on their feet, camcorders in hand, photographing each other on the pitch of this World Cup semi-final which they were about to play against Brazil, as delighted as me to be there, and going to chat with their supporters, crammed into the north curve where a sea of red and blue flags had just opened up. Then the Brazilians casually appeared on the pitch, in little groups of three or four, wearing their strange blue training vests over their jerseys, the three goalkeepers wearing an identical kit that looked like greyish flannelette pyjamas, and they started warming up gently, passing the ball offhandedly to one another under the bright floodlights of the Saitama stadium, lit up in the night. It was with placid delight and contained emotion that I finally recognised through the sights of my binoculars, among the players stretching there on the pitch, the familiar faces of Ronaldo and Rivaldo, which gave me the feeling, as it did every time I saw Brazil moving around a stadium, of seeing before me a timeless Brazilian team where Jaïrzinho rubbed shoulders with Roberto Carlos, Tostao with Ronaldinho, under the emblematic and tutelary shadow of Edson Arantes do Nascimento, better known by the name of Pelé.

If, at this World Cup, I faithfully supported Belgium and briefly France, it's always Brazil that I carry in my heart when it comes to football – what would football be if it weren't for Brazil? – with its artistic play, its technique and its grace, its lightness and speed, with its immemorial yellow and green and its colourful supporters, its carnival queens in bikinis with gold tiaras in their hair, their bare bellies and their skin tanned and palpitating in the summer evening, from whom I stood a few inches away in the dampness of Kobe Stadium. The game wasn't yet over when already, from the top of the stands, the carnival got going, drums at the front, and started to come down the stands sweeping aside everything in its path, Japanese supporters and security staff overwhelmed, to go and dance an endless samba beside the pitch, where the eleven legendary yellow jerseys went on sliding endlessly like waves on to the pitch and into the marvelling imaginations of children all over the world.

*

When, at exactly 10 o'clock on the night of 30 June 2002, Pierluigi Collina called time on the match between Brazil and Germany in the World Cup final, I got to my feet in the stands along with my neighbours and raised my arms to the heavens. Wedged into my folding seat in the north stand since the beginning of the match, I had followed the clash between a middle-aged Spanish-speaking couple and two dark young people with the build of the Indian subcontinent, stocky and beefy, bare-chested under low-necked white sleeveless T-shirts (sometimes we over-idealise mythical finals), divided between my enlightened enthusiasm for the Brazilian game and my legitimate affection for the European cause. On the pitch, already invaded by photographers and officials running in all directions, by crestfallen Germans and euphoric Brazilians praying on the ground and waving flags, hordes of Japanese volunteers in green overalls hastily set up a makeshift platform, and, when Cafu, the Brazilian captain, picked up the trophy and brandished it in front of the crowd, a huge cheer rang out around the stadium, with a rain of sequins and a bubble of smoke canisters fired by silver cannons, while in the terraces a deluge of multicoloured paper filigrees suddenly fell from the roofs and inundated the stands where everyone, standing up and clapping, raised their arms to wave them away, catch them in mid-air or gather them up in their hands.

Now, at home, as relics of the final, I have three of these Japanese papers, which I have carefully chosen in the colours of Brazil: yellow, green and blue.

Leaving the terraces, while I walked along the massive silhouette of the huge concrete building of Yokohama Stadium, a disagreeable drizzle began to fall, light at first, then more and more persistent. I stopped for a moment and opened my backpack to take out a transparent raincoat, which had not yet left its original wrapping. I had bought it in Kobe two weeks earlier, hours before the Brazil-Belgium match, fearing some tropical storm that might have soaked me to the skin, and I now took it with me to every match. I put it on over my clothes and, armoured with this transparent raincoat that covered me entirely from head to toe, I set off again into the night, following the slow and docile crowd that snaked between two lines of stewards and policemen who pointed us the way in the darkness with the ends of their fluorescent truncheons, they too covered by a panoply of transparent raincoats. It was a strange procession that moved like that through the damp night of Yokohama towards the metro, swept from time to time by the yellow glow of a few taxis or a bus headlamp manoeuvring in the distance to leave the car parks. Reaching the foot of the elevated metro at Kozukue, we had to slow down, blocked by a cordon of police, and came to a standstill for a few minutes in front of the bottleneck at the only entrance, the police allowing us to reach the escalators only in a sequence of waves. At the top of the stairs, in the metro station where the crowd hurried to the ticket counters and shook out their umbrellas in a damp haze of public baths, I began to step forward clumsily in my all-over transparent plastic outfit that looked like a post-Chernobyl or pre-Fukushima overall, when, looking in a circle around the room I recognized, three metres away from me, leaning against a wall near the ticket counters, my friend Romano Tommasini, violinist with the Berlin Philharmonic, who was absently watching the crowd passing. Striding towards him, still completely trammelled up in my dripping outfit, I threw myself into his arms (hoping that it was him, and not just some guy waiting peacefully), delighted and disbelieving, like a reunion scene in an Italian comedy. Romano! I exclaimed, hugging him. We were still marvelling at this extraordinary coincidence which had led us to meet by chance at the exit of the stadium amidst this crowd of eighty thousand people, when a Japanese gentleman who seemed to be trying to find his way, came cautiously over to me and said in a low voice in French, 'Excuse me, but I was at your lecture yesterday evening at the Institut Français, and I asked a question, remember?'

One of the marvellous revelations of this World Cup were the Japanese spectators. While in Europe most football supporters are male, violent, racist, full of beer or wine, in Japan the spectators are gentle and refined, sensitive, intelligent and cultivated or, to put it another way, in Europe football is a man's game, while in Japan it's more, as on shipwrecks, women and children first. You go there as a couple or a family, amongst friends and even amongst girls. I was struck by the number of girls on their own who were on their way to the stadium, with the big blue jersey of the Japanese team, too big for them, floating around their shoulders and falling to their thighs, and they were experiencing the event like a playful, pacifist game, a kind of gala, a firework display, a mega concert where the rock stars were called things like Nakata and Beckham. In the metro, I even made the acquaintance of a four-and-a-half-year-old girl who was being taken to the game by her father (slightly intimidated, she began by staring at me with her big black eyes, before smiling when I began photographing her, and getting up on the banquette on her knees, a pennant in her hand, with her tiny Japanese flag painted on her cheek). Then I think again of all those Japanese I had met for a moment during this World Cup, with whom I swapped a glance, a smile, who photographed me or whose photograph I took – little girl on the metro, but also laughing girls taking photographs of themselves, a young father I bumped into on the terraces with a baby in his arms, both wearing a blue Ono jersey, or that young bare-chested Japanese man in Kobe with a Belgian flag tattooed on his biceps – I see again all those people from the organizing committee, boys and girls all jumbled together, wearing their fluid fluorescent yellow plastic overalls bearing the black letters STEWARD, searching through bags at the entrance and who were seen again at the exit forming a line of honour for the spectators and saying goodbye to them, smiling and waving, or those hundreds of extras at the closing ceremony that I happened upon, their performance finished and apparently successful, congratulating one another and skipping on the spot like children in the shade of a giant concrete pillar at Yokohama Stadium. I think again of all those faces I spotted for a moment, in trains and stadiums, of all those poignant, vanished hours now drifting away in time and starting to blur in my memory.

*

49

We're in the early 1990s, it's my first trip to Japan, and I'm looking at the Kamo through the bamboo blinds of the window of my room at the Fujita Hotel. The sky is grey, the river bed is almost dry, the water barely flows between the short grass and the pebbles. It seemed so ugly to me, the Kamo that I love so much today, the first time I saw it. It's more than ten years now that I've been watching the Kamo flow like an image of passing time, identical and different, day and night, under the sun or under the rain. I'm in Kyoto again now. I walk on the deserted banks near Demachiyanagi, I cross a bridge, the river is almost in spate, it's a torrent, I stop on the slope under my transparent umbrella and look at the seething water, the flood, the whirlpool – and, for the first time, the course of time strikes me as threatening. I look at the Kamo, and time growls, passing along with the water: I'm ageing with the rhythm of its course.

GERMANY, 2006

For the 2006 World Cup in Germany I decided to
go and see all the games being played in Berlin.
Six matches were due in Berlin's Olympic stadium,
Brazil-Croatia, Sweden-Paraguay, Germany-Ecuador,
Ukraine-Tunisia, the quarter-final and the final. I or-
dered a ticket for each game online and, a few days later,
I had a reply from a guy at the ticketing centre who, in
passable albeit slightly stiff Franglais, gave me a user
name and a password (xbh_SG1_Z, you're never going
to forget that). I paid, or promised to pay, a fortune, and
I waited for the tickets thinking about something else
(poetry, perhaps). In the end I didn't get a SINGLE
ticket for a SINGLE match. Full. Sold out. *Ausverkauft*.
For all the games in the 2006 World Cup, the Olympic
Stadium in Berlin was inaccessible. A supplementary
draw, a repechage, like the *consolante*, the extra tournament in boules (at which I generally excel), was
organized and I won a place, a timid establishment of
contact with the history of the World Cup, perhaps not
the seat of my dreams, but access to the Grail: a seat for
Sweden-Paraguay on 15 June (in sporting terms it's a bit
like the group of death: no one survived).

On the day of the game I showed up very early to take
advantage of every last minute of my precious ticket's
validity, and strolled peacefully down the still quiet avenues of the *Olympiastadion*, clutching a transparent cup of
beer and balancing a bratwurst that reeled dangerously
towards the mustard in a curved cardboard tray. Lost
in my thoughts, I stopped here and there in front of the
panels explaining in English and German the history of
the stadium, pausing in front of the 1936 Olympic pool,

which I observed through the grilles as I nibbled on my bratwurst. I was wearing a black T-shirt and a black linen jacket, backpack over my shoulder, my beloved red BELGIUM cap back in the wardrobe of disillusion since the elimination of Belgium in the preliminary phase (I had left it in Brussels, what would I have done with a BELGIUM cap on my head for a Sweden-Paraguay game?) I could certainly have rivalled one of a considerable number of off-topic spectators: a lot of Brazilian and German jerseys around me in the hallways, some Australian sun hats, Mexican jumpers, Dutch scarves, Japanese caps and even one guy with a Peru jersey; I could have shaken his hand, assured him of my sympathy as another supporter of an eliminated country. The hallways were filling up with Swedes, thousands of Swedes in yellow jerseys, sometimes blue ones, with the inscription SVERIGE, Viking caps, faces painted blue, with pennants, ribbons, headbands, charms, trumpets, yellow and blue wigs, Swedish girls with little flags tattooed on their cheeks, their foreheads, their shoulders, their forearms, their calves (and elsewhere too, I imagine, but I wasn't given the opportunity to check). I walked among this increasingly noisy compact yellow crowd, and I must admit that I didn't notice at first, but it struck me all of a sudden that I was the only guy in the stadium wearing a jacket. I ended up getting rid of the jacket, come on (it was just under 30 in the shade in Berlin, beneath the imposing neo-classical columns of the Olympic stadium), and went to find my seat in the west curve, by the Marathon Arch. I was perched quite high up at the top of the stadium, beneath the big stone clock (out of order, apparently, the sole hieratic hand didn't move an inch during the whole game, it was the only thing to remain phlegmatic in the surrounding area). A few minutes before kick-off, the last unoccupied seats filling inexorably with belated Swedes, two particularly special Swedish individuals came and sat beside me, bewigged, tattooed, daubed, loaded down with flags and rattles, already drunk, over-excited, a boy and a girl with whom I had had extremely remote relations throughout the game, a minimalist cordiality for a constrained cohabitation on our narrow seats, until the final goal by the Swedes, which broke the ice in the 89th minute of the game and when, in his exuberant, expansive and muddle-headed joy, the guy, my neighbour (let's call him Sven, if you like), having embraced everyone within range, his companion first of all, then the Swedes sitting in front of him, having no one left to celebrate the winning goal with and not knowing where to put his expansionist impulses, threw himself into my arms and hugged me in the stadium stands as I have rarely been hugged (even though I was supporting Paraguay).

SOUTH AFRICA, 2010

Perhaps people thought I was joking, but it's true, I am beginning to get a bit fed up with football. And besides, I'm not going to say anything about this 2010 World Cup. Not a word about South Africa.

At Le Mans, since I was in Le Mans (the World Cup, for me, in 2010, began in the Sarthe), I felt as if I was abroad, perhaps because everyone around me was speaking English or German. I felt as if I was in a permanent state of jet lag, which happens to me increasingly often, everywhere in the world, where I always feel 'that slight distortion in the order of reality, that gap, that twist, that basic mismatch between the world, however familiar, that we have in front of our eyes and the remote, distant way in which we perceive it.' I must admit that I had something to do with it. At about nine in the evening, coming back to the hotel for the first time since the start of the race, exhausted as a racing driver, my eyes small, stinging, sleepy, my ears humming, my big laminated pass that I was wearing casually around my neck, my cap on crooked, engine oil on my hands and my chin (I'm exaggerating a bit, perhaps it was just some chocolate mousse from the VIP room) – all that was missing from the racing-driver look was the fireproof overall with plastron and reinforced elbows – I approach reception – a very cosy French provincial hotel, a young woman in a blue suit behind the counter (Le Mans, basically, the French provinces, a film by Chabrol, the smell of boeuf bourguignon simmering in a kitchen somewhere out of shot). I put my backpack down heavily on the counter, take off my sweat-pickled cap, I'm exhausted after six hours of driving, and I say to the young woman: 'I'm going to take a little siesta.' She looks at me, slightly surprised. 'Can you wake me up at ten o'clock?' I say. I become more specific: 'Ten o'clock in the evening' (because in the provinces you don't have a siesta at nine o'clock in the evening, or anywhere else in the world, for that matter). She records my wishes in a big notebook, she nods, got that, and I go back to my room. I close the curtains, because in June it's still daylight in the Sarthe at nine in the evening – you would think you were in Helsinki – I turn on the television and, distractedly, as I start casually undressing in my room to go and take a shower, I notice that England are winning 1-0 against the United States at the Royal Bafokeng Stadium in Rustenburg. Because if the 24 hours of Le Mans began six hours ago, that means it's already more than twenty-four hours – what symmetry – since the football World Cup began in South Africa and since, for the moment, I haven't seen a single game (barely a picture in passing the previous evening, in the restaurant, during the first French game, when I got up for a moment during the reception dinner given in honour of Jeff Koons).

Jeff Koons: I had spent twenty-four hours living more or less with him, admitted into his immediate entourage, like a barely identified far-off satellite (I'm not sure if he really knew who I was). In general I gravitated alone in my corner a little way away from the artistic and Koonish effervescence that he provoked, occasionally altering my orbit with a slight cautious ellipsoid approach curve (sometimes geostationary, which isn't a good sign), to exchange a few words with him in the streets of Le Mans (about his recent travels, particularly to Beijing, where he was preparing an exhibition). Far

58

from his elegant grey Savile-Row-style suits and sober tie that we see him wearing in recent photographs, that evening in Le Mans Jeff Koons was wearing quite a tight red-wine coloured polo shirt (which looked a little like a pyjama jacket), and he cordially answered my questions as we made our way to the restaurant. With a youthful face and fine, studious wire-framed glasses, he is an open and sympathetic man (for twenty-four hours he complied with all requests – questions, photographs, signatures – with remarkable generosity, a constant smile and the patience of an angel). He told me he was coming back from China, and that he always took his whole family with him, his wife and his four children, four tow-headed little ones, all boys, from two to ten, uniformly dressed in identical T-shirts, blue one day, red the next (he also had one of these tow-headed little ones in his arms while we were speaking, trying to set him down at a red light, but being obliged to pick him up in response to the little boy's vehement protests), not to mention a baby on the way in his wife's belly (a girl, apparently – congratulations, Jeff) and two babysitters (I'm not forgetting anyone). All these lovely people were running in between the legs of the BMW PR men and journalists, climbing on to tables and shouting, babbling, calling out to each other and pinching each other, kicking one another's shins, complaining and whining, beneath the affectionate smiles of the press attachés, while Dad (Pops) went on signing autographs with Zen detachment (wondering whether he might be able to keep the noise-cancelling headphones that he'd been given for the 24 Hours of Le Mans).

After my siesta (at about eleven o'clock), a driver from the organization came to get me from the hotel and I went back towards the circuit of the 24 Hours of Le Mans. Night had just fallen, and I snoozed in the front of the car, my backpack on my knees. We hadn't yet reached the circuit, we hadn't yet seen a single car on the track, when the noise arose somewhere in the distance, came closer to us and suddenly enveloped us in its pure violence – the infernal noise of racing cars passing, invisible, in the night – that noise that isn't like any other, always the same sequence of identical sounds, rising engine power, the paroxysmal summit of the roar, then a few last sputters, the decreasing put-puts at the end of the straight. We were still a few hundred metres from the official entrance, which we sensed behind the high barbed-wire walls of the circuit, when, having straightened a little in my seat, I spotted through the windscreen a firework display from the big car parks that line the circuit, an amateur firework display, two or three sluggish rockets inundating the sky with a slow motion shower of spangles. I watched the rockets bursting softly and almost silently in the sky, and I imagined that this unlikely firework display – as if fired off by extras to prepare my metaphor – was celebrating the movement along the track of Art Car by Jeff Koons.

I would see it coming from a long way off in the night, Jeff Koons' Art Car, preceded by its headlights and the mounting roar of the engine, emerging into the Corvette Curves to accelerate and slide at top speed along the high wire fence protecting the track where the marshals stand, with their reflective yellow vests, frail motionless silhouettes rooted to the spot by the speed of the cars passing like lightning in front of their eyes and slipping horizontally into the night with a noise of thunder. It wasn't a car that I would see passing, but a luminous concept in motion, the whole of the electro-magnetic spectrum merged together and fluidified by speed in a symphony of multi-coloured spangles, segments of broken lines, a shower of pure colours, dazzling, acidulous, the orange, the yellow, the green, the blue, slipping horizontally into the night, autonomous, free as will-o-the-wisps, the launch of an idea of power and energy, the furtive passage of an incandescent meteor of colour and fire. That was what I thought I would see as the Art Car passed: a firework display of colours in the night.

But on reaching the circuit I was told that the Art Car had given up. After barely eight hours of racing it was all over, they were probably wrapping it up right now like a vulgar Christo. Jeff Koons had gone back to the hotel (very disappointed, apparently). And I was disappointed too. I had nothing more to do at the 24 Hours of Le Mans, and I didn't linger (before two o'clock in the morning I was back at the hotel). I don't know if Jeff Koons had had time to change, or if he was still wearing his splendid white padded driver's overalls that he had been given to wear to watch the race, with a full-colour reminder of the car on the back, like a giant Paul Smith label, the same brightly coloured vertical lines. We could have had one last glass together in the deserted bar of this *manceau* hotel to soften our disappointment, each on his high stool, in this subdued provincial hotel with its fading lights.

BRAZIL, 2014

I went through some difficult times in early 2014. My
father died in December 2013, and in *Nue* I had just
completed a sequence of novels that had kept me busy
for over ten years. A cycle was coming to an end, leaving me empty and lost. I experienced a crisis, a fleeting
moment of doubt, uncertainty and dejection, which led
me to inquire into the meaning of my life and my com-
mitment to literature.

It was then, in the summer of 2014, during or just
after the football World Cup, that, twice, fireflies crossed my path. The first time, a real firefly, a glow worm
glimpsed suddenly in the night. It was one evening, late,
near the bins, I glimpsed a firefly in the darkness of
a hot June evening in Corsica, a little streamer of luminescent green, crystalline and liquid, which sent out its
fragile, motionless signal on the slope of a hill, between
the grass and the rocks plunging into the darkness. The
second time it was the immaterial fireflies in the book
by Georges Didi-Huberman. I discovered *Survivance des
lucioles* (*Survival of the Fireflies*) by chance in June at the
Palais de Tokyo bookshop, and reading it gave me the
kind of unexpected happiness that the sudden appearance of a firefly in the night can yield, a little miraculous
rarity, a fortuitous encounter that irradiates the mind
and illuminates the darkness with its frail luminescent
stimulation.

What does it mean to create, today, in the world we
live in? It means proposing, now and again, an act of
resistance that is not modest, but minor, a signal – a
book, a work of art – which will send out a faint, vain

and wanton light into the night. I had been revolving for several months around this idea, this inquiry, these questions, and for me Didi-Huberman's book was that firefly. What Didi-Huberman's book allowed me to understand was that the problem wasn't the darkness of the world that surrounded me, on the contrary, it was its excess of brightness. What I was doing in stubbornly pursuing my work as a writer for thirty years was simply forcing myself to assert a possible human path, a way, an attitude, a delicacy, a subtlety, a gentleness, a dignity. Which, in terms of immediate advantages – glory, money, fame, in short everything that weighs down on even the least significant football star – mightn't bring me much, but which would serve as an example to my children and, through them, to future generations, to the human race as a whole. In spite of the difficulties, in spite of the harshness of the task, I had to persevere. Not deviate from my path, stay away from the hubbub and agitation of the world. Not allow myself to be dazzled by the blinding brightness of the *fierce* floodlights evoked by Didi-Huberman, 'the floodlights of watchtowers, of political shows, of football stadiums, of television platforms', not that I reject light or fear it. But in order to create I need shadow, silence and solitude.

At the end of his book, Georges Didi-Huberman mentions Hannah Arendt's book *On Humanity in Dark Times*, and I retain the phrase 'dark times', which spreads like a soothing balm over my despondency. In general I don't like jeremiads, and avoid making disparaging judgements about the age (even when I have toothache). I would remind the moaners who complain about their times of Beckett's quotation in *Waiting for Godot*: 'There's man all over for you, blaming on his boots the faults of his feet.' But I admit that the times are dark, today, in Europe. Where is the ideal? We are lulled by false pretences, our points of reference elude us, even the beams from the most powerful headlights turn without leaving a trace in the blinding light of vulgarity – so what's to be said about the fragile lights of fireflies? As Hannah Arendt says, man is in the situation of someone confronted with an age in which 'the public realm has lost the power of illumination'. An age 'in which we no longer feel "enlightened" according to the order of reasons nor "radiant" according to the order of affects'. And Georges Didi-Huberman concludes: 'So this is what some people, in such a situation, will have chosen to do: withdraw "from the world" of *light* while working on something that might "still be useful to the world", a *gleam*, in short.'

I didn't write a word about the World Cup in South Africa, and I thought this year I would skip over the World Cup in Brazil as well. I spent the summer of 2014 in Corsica, in the house in Barcaggio where there is no television and where, until last year, we had neither telephone nor internet. I thought that this 2014 World Cup would play out without me, that it would, in short, be marked essentially by absence. The absence of my father first of all (this World Cup is the first one to play without him), and perhaps also, as an unconscious echo, by my own absence, my voluntary withdrawal from the world to devote myself to writing, my disappearance, my eclipse into the night. So the World Cup in Brazil started without me, I wasn't physically present in São Paulo on 12 June 2014 for the opening match, or in front of a television, not even near a radio. However there is, as I very well know, an outmoded charm in listening to a football match on the radio, as I did in Corsica, in 2003, for that Champions League match between Juventus and AC Milan which I followed on the radio lying on my bed, the shutters open on to a spring night. But no, it was literature, and literature alone, that I planned to devote myself to that summer. I've always been in search of a closed place, cut off from the world, warm, reassuring, a place of dreams that might have assumed the image of a bathroom in my first book, but which could now no longer be anything else than literature itself. It was into literature that I intended to withdraw that summer, and to sum myself up in it, to merge with it.

Two kinds of faint depression accompanied the writing of the novels in the Marie cycle: that the book I was writing did not come up to my expectations (while it might have been good, it certainly wasn't as good as it could have been, not as good as I'd have dreamed it might be), and that, on the contrary, it was very good, but so good, in fact, that by comparison the real world lost all of its savour, that I had reached such aquatic depths while writing it, that I had travelled through such underwater territories, distant, dark, enchanting, that I had made such discoveries within myself and that I was coming back bearing such treasures that the real world couldn't help but disappoint me when I came back up to the surface. Out of the water, away from writing and its enchantments, not to mention its demands, its discipline, the real world would soon leave me dissatisfied, and I then very quickly felt a *disappointment with the world*. But that disappointment, that dark dissatisfaction that was with me when I wasn't writing – that left me stretched out on my bed, unemployed, in my socks (you know me) – was precisely the incentive that I needed to get back to work. Then I got back to it and started writing again, and the disappointment of the world disappeared to leave me once again facing doubt, silence and uncertainty, that dark unease that always goes hand in hand with writing.

When I'm not writing, it seems to me that the day-to-day experiences that I have confronted in my life, the happy ones, but most of all the painful ones, the ones that flay or wound me, happen to me in vain. They slide over my life, they don't leave a mark, they have nothing to attach themselves to, they happen as they might happen to a tree, my beloved olive tree in the little garden. Conversely, when a book is in progress, everything comes to my aid, everything is useful to me, I grab everything within my reach to take advantage of it. At every hour of the day, whether I am walking on the beach or strolling up the path through the scrubland to the old tower, whether I'm swimming in the sea or reading in the little garden, when I'm sleeping, a tireless process of ripening is still at work. Even if I'm not physically writing anything at my computer, the book has been launched, the writing is under way. Unlike the periods in my life when I'm not writing, the new project, however early it is in its development, however rudimentary its outline, becomes the magnet, or the mooring, where the thousands of nutritious substances that I glean around me from the outside world mass together like mussels on a mussel-bed, while the new book, fertilised by these accumulated contributions, is already starting to grow and spread in my mind.

*

The view that faces me in the big room of the house in Barcaggio is immutable, the two turquoise armchairs and the little garden, in the axis of my gaze, which can be seen through the window. This is where I write, when I'm in Corsica, in this room which used to be the classroom of the local school (the house was the old village school), and I have a feeling that the atmosphere is still imbued with certain images from my books, as if the room had preserved the secret memory of the hours of work spent here. Without being superstitious, I think places can give off beneficial waves, that certain places are more conducive than others to lovemaking or artistic creation, because of an abolished past that goes on inhabiting them, as if some immaterial traces of their story still floated in the atmosphere. The invisible waves which emanate in this way from the young Corsican schoolchildren who studied in this room in the late 1950s have, since I've been writing here myself, been joined by the impalpable vestiges of images from my books. I look up from my computer, and already, gently, in the empty room stretching out in front of me, I can see the Place Saint-Sulpice slowly appearing, rising up in my mind like a theatre set from the past that's starting to fill the room with its mute presence. As if the image of the square that I summoned in this very office in 1986 were returning to life by immersing itself once again in the spring that saw its birth, the mind that created it, I see assembling before my eyes the marble outlines of the church, the flagstones of the square, the curved basins of the Visconti Fountain, which come to life for a moment in front of me before almost immediately dissolving into the limbo of memory. All of these images, fed on my past and loaded with literary labour, gorged with emotions and saturated with memories, that now assail me all at once. This ancient rain, fixed as if for ever in the avenues of time, which goes on falling in slow motion in my memory, endlessly crossing the bright halo of a floodlight at New Haven Marine railway station. It's this line of coiled, red lanterns that constantly accompanies the flight by motorcycle of the characters in *Fuir*, it's the thoroughbred Zahir galloping, motionless, on the tarmac of Narita airport before disappearing slowly into memory. I feel that all these intimate images go on floating here in suspension in the air, not materially, like the damp or saltpetre that impregnate the walls, but invisibly, in the aura of the place that they saturate with buried memories and vanished sensations. But it is here, this summer, on these literary images slumbering in the atmosphere of the big room in the house in Barcaggio, that *incompatible* images – concrete, base, rough and prosaic – have come to superimpose themselves, trivial images, profane images: images of football.

Here, this summer, a genuine short circuit took place, a sacrilegious collision, the inopportune superimposition of images that are fundamentally different in nature. It is as if a sly and devastating virus had managed to slip into my work-place, this room protected from the outside world where the fragile and poetic images of my books are born and, having weakened my defences, neutralized my resistance and paralysed my creative activity, have managed to take control of my work tool and infected my computer. It was here, on the very computer on which I write my books, that I first watched a football match on live stream.

But how did I come to watch a football match on live stream (even though, until then, I hadn't even known the expression, let alone the technique), and even though for over a week I had scrupulously stayed away from this World Cup that had just begun in Brazil to devote myself exclusively to literature? I don't know. Perhaps it's the fact that, very early in the morning, at about half past six, in the sleeping house in Barcaggio, when I tiptoed into my deserted office, with my cup of coffee, sitting down at the big oak table to start working, I began by connecting to the internet to pick up the night's emails and, while I was at it, my God, what's the harm, before starting, I took a quick glance at the matches that had been played in Brazil the previous day. But only to catch the scores, nothing more than that. It was, I fear, however, the first rash act, the first guilty slackening of vigilance. Then, one thing leading to another, and since the newspapers and the radio stations no longer mentioned anything but this World Cup – already with its first highlights: the litigious victory of Brazil in the opening match, or the fleeting success of Italy against England in the damp night of Manaus – I took another step closer and found out about the different legal offers of streamed broadcasts, and by rummaging about a little, good heavens, I subscribed to beIN SPORTS CONNECT. The principle is very simple: you pay a fee of €12 for all the matches in the World Cup, you choose a user name and a password, you download the Silverlight software and, when the match comes around, almost in real time, you receive the continuous video flow at a resolution of 720p on your computer, with an imperceptible gap, a breath, a delay of about 25 seconds from digital television.

So it was on my own, in the big room in the house in Barcaggio, that I watched the semi-final which set the Netherlands against Argentina in this 2014 World Cup. The ceremonial aspect, the arrangement, remained the same, I had set up my laptop computer on the sofa in the room, raising it like an offering on a profane little altar consisting of two or three volumes of the Encyclopédie Universalis (a paradoxical homage of virtue to vice), and I sat down opposite the sofa, sliding along the floor one of the two turquoise armchairs which I placed in front of the screen. But in fact, what I was watching there, on live stream on my computer since the beginning of the World Cup, were matches which, independently of the real weather conditions prevailing in Brazil, invariably played out in fog. From time to time, after a hiccup in the picture and a brief pause in the broadcast, everything stopped and the sibylline message appeared in the middle of the screen: *buffering* (in English, in italics and preceded by three little dots). The application was trying to find a second wind, or fresh inspiration and, after a brief gargle, an electronic baby-burp, the game resumed as it might have done after a throw-in, almost in the same place where I had left it (sometimes, in the interval, a goal had been scored). Often, too, the ball disappeared completely from view into the bright pix-elated pea purée of the electronic nebuliser that I had in front of my eyes. It happened, for example, every time the camera did a panoramic shot, and on practically all the set pieces, on free kicks and corners. There was something that resembled a very dynamic ellipsis in the editing, and you immediately arrived at the result of the move, the shot that failed or was repelled by the defence, or, still more radically, every now and again, the goal-keeper going to get the ball from the back of the net – an unquestionable sign that a goal had been scored. Who by was a mystery. But you still saw it a bit better than you did on the radio (and I didn't deny my pleasure).

That evening, because of the time difference, the match had begun at ten o'clock in the evening, and Madeleine had gone upstairs to bed, she was reading or listening to the radio up there. I had turned out all the lights in the room, and allowed myself to be carried along by the match, sitting in my turquoise armchair. Not a great deal was happening on the pitch, the two teams were paralysed by the high stakes, trying not to let goals in rather than trying to score one themselves. I don't know what time it could have been, it was already quite far into the night, and the game seemed to be heading straight for extra time. The wind had risen up outside, I could hear the shutters creaking on their hinges behind the windows. Every time I noticed a flash of lightning through the window, momentarily lighting up the room with a ghostly white glow, I couldn't help doing what I have always done since childhood (I was already doing it at the age of nine in Sart-Dames-Avelines) and mentally counting out the number of seconds from the moment when you notice the lightning to the one when you hear the thunder. With each new thunderclap I imagined the wind blowing up a storm in the night, agitating the scrubland and twisting the shrubs on their trunks. At the Tour d'Agnello, at the top of the path, the clouds must have been massing over the hill and passing the ridge line amid dazzling flashes. I'm very familiar with the path that leads to the old tower, it's the one I take every time I go for a stroll. Up there, once you reach the top, the horizon opens up in all directions on to the Ligurian Sea, Capraia is visible in the distance, the Gorgone, and sometimes the Isle of Elba, if the weather is good. But this evening all that anyone could see would be clouds on the horizon, black, threatening clouds coming from the sea and flocking into the sky to make their way towards the village.

Meanwhile in Brazil, Argentina and the Netherlands hadn't managed to reach a decision at the end of extra time, and we were getting ready to proceed to the penalty shoot-out. Sitting in the gloom, I went on watching the live stream of the match on my laptop on the sofa. The atmosphere at the ground was very oppressive, the players were sitting on the pitch in semi-circles, hands on the ground behind them, being given massages, their socks lowered, the trainers were passing among the little groups before proceeding to the selection of the first five shooters. The storm was still rumbling in the distance, and there was an unfamiliar electrical activity in the room. Then the first alert appeared on my computer screen, a sudden drop in power and then, at the precise moment when the first Dutch player was coming forward to shoot, the image froze completely, followed by a total interruption of the live stream and a break pure and simple in the internet connection. I had lost the picture on my computer at the very moment when it had become captivating, just as the penalty shoot-out was about to begin. I looked around for help, totally at a loss, I bent over the computer and moved it, I turned it on its axis, as I might have shifted an old television with an aerial to get back reception (you can tell that I lived through the twentieth century). Then, pulling myself together, I hastily tried to reconnect to the internet, I entered all my connection codes, my user name and my password to get back to beIN SPORTS. I waited, anxious and impotent (it was, after all, a place in the World Cup final that was at stake). I saw quite clearly that it wasn't going to work, and hurried out of the office, walked a little way down the corridor, turned on my heels, no longer knew what I was doing, I tried to find a way to follow the penalty shoot-out which must already have started in Brazil. In the kitchen I turned on the old radio that is always plugged into the mains, and happened upon a France Info presenter who was busy explaining, live from the Arena in São Paulo, that it was Robben's turn to shoot for the Netherlands. Bent over the old radio, I listened to the report, my eyes lost in the distance, tense, concentrating, tying to visualize what was happening on the pitch. The storm had got even worse, the rain hammered down on the roof and rumbles of thunder, closer and closer – then a violent, precise, roaring crash: lightning had just struck the lane outside. I saw the light from the bulb flickering on the ceiling, and all of a sudden the radio broadcast halted, and all the lights in the house went out. The electricity had been cut off.

I was in complete darkness. I felt my way down the corridor and went back into the big room to confirm that nothing was working, not the electricity or the internet connection. I climbed the stairs four at a time to get to the first floor, went into the bedroom without making a sound to keep from waking Madeleine, and picked up a little battery transistor off the chest of drawers. I went back down to the ground floor, turning on the little transistor while I was still on the stairs, at first found only the crackles of the frequency modulation, sometimes scraps of advertisements or Italian music. I was twisting the tuning button on the transistor as I went into the big room, when at last I found an Italian radio station that was broadcasting the match, but I was a little lost, I couldn't quite work out where they were in the penalty shoot-out, what the score was, who was leading and who was about to shoot, and the Italian commentator went on talking, voluble, precise, quick, passionate, stirring the audience with his rushing phrases, when all of a sudden I worked out the situation, what was at stake, the ultimate suspense, it was Maxi Rodriguez's turn to shoot, the commentator explained, and hence, it was very simple, if he scored, it was over, Argentina was through. At that precise moment, nothing could reach me, no power cut or break in the internet connection, only a sudden expiry of the transistor battery could have deprived me of this final moment of suspense. I was there, a little transistor at my ear, standing in the room where I normally write my books, and then, in the night, I heard the yell of enthusiastic confirmation from this Italian presenter – who was this man, who was he addressing in the night like this? – who was shouting himself hoarse in Italian about how Maxi Rodriguez had got the ball in the net! That Argentina were in the final! That it was Argentina that would be facing Germany in the 2014 World Cup final!

The electricity still hadn't come back on in the village when I joined Madeleine in the bedroom, about ten minutes later. I had opened the window and parted the shutters, and stepped out on to the balcony to look at the village in the night again for a moment. All the houses were still plunged in darkness. The night was silent, the rain had stopped, the branches of the trees dripped slowly on the wet tarmac of the square. The storms were still raging in Italy, and I studied the veiled turmoil in the sky on the line of the horizon, which I saw torn by jolts, in whitish palpitations, shaking and mute. Then weakly, behind me, I heard the sleepy voice of Madeleine in her bed, asking me gently, 'Is the football over?' Yes, it was over.

Now it's the sky.

ZIDANE'S MELANCHOLY

Zidane looked at the sky over Berlin without thinking about anything, a white sky dappled with blue-grey clouds, one of those vast, changing, windy skies that you see in Flemish paintings, Zidane looked at the sky above the Olympic stadium on the evening of 9 July 2006, and he experienced with heartrending intensity the feeling of simply being there, in the Olympic Stadium in Berlin, at that precise moment, the evening of the World Cup final.

It was probably only a matter of form and melancholy on the evening of the final. First of all, immediately, form in its pure state, the penalty converted in the seventh minute, an indolent Panenka which touched the crossbar before crossing the line and coming back out of the goal, a billiard-ball trajectory already flirting with Geoff Hurst's legendary shot at Wembley in 1966. But it was still just a quotation, an involuntary homage to a legendary episode from the World Cup. Zidane's true gesture on the evening of that final – a sudden gesture like an outburst of black bile in the lonely night – will only happen much later, and erase the rest, the end of the game and the extra time, the penalty kicks and the winner, a decisive gesture, violent, prosaic and romantic: a perfect moment of ambiguity beneath the Berlin sky, a few dizzying seconds of ambivalence, in which beauty and blackness, violence and passion, come into contact and create a short circuit with an original gesture.

Zidane's headbutt had all the suddenness and finesse of a calligraphic gesture. If it only took a few seconds to perform, it could only have happened at the end of a slow maturation process, a long genesis, invisible and secret. Zidane's gesture is unaware of the aesthetic categories of the beautiful or the sublime, it lies beyond the moral categories of good and evil, its value, its strength and its substance have to do only with their appropriateness, irreducible to the precise moment when it occurred. Two vast subterranean currents must have carried it from very far away, the first, fundamental one, broad, silent, powerful, inexorable, which flows as much from pure melancholy as it does from the sorrowful perception of the passing of time, is bound up with the sadness of the announcement of the end, the bitterness of the player disputing the last match of his career and unable to bring himself to finish. Zidane has never been able to bring himself to finish, he is familiar with stage exits (against Greece), or bad endings (against South Korea). It has never been possible for him to bring his career to an end, and even, and particularly, to go out in a blaze of glory, because going out in a blaze of glory is still ending the legend: to brandish the World Cup is to accept death, while a bad ending leaves perspectives open, unknown and alive. The other current that carried his gesture along, a parallel and contradictory current, fed on an excess of black bile and Saturnine influences, is the desire to get things over with as quickly as possible, the irrepressible desire to leave the pitch abruptly and go to the changing room (*I left abruptly, without telling anybody*[I]), because the weariness is there, sudden, immeasurable, the weariness, the exhaustion, the painful shoulder, Zidane can't score, he's had enough of his partners, he's had enough of the world and himself. Zidane's melancholy is my melancholy, I know, I've fed it and I feel it. The world becomes opaque, your limbs are heavy, *the hours seemed weighted, slower, interminable*[II]. He feels sly and he becomes vulnerable. *Something inside turns against us*[III] – and, drunk with exhaustion and nervous tension, Zidane can't carry out the liberating act of violence, or relieving flight, he is otherwise incapable of undoing the nervous tension that oppresses him (and it is the *final flight from the completion of the work*[IV]). Besides, since the start of extra time, Zidane never stopped giving unconscious expression to his weariness with his captain's armband which kept slipping down, his armband which was coming to pieces, and which he kept awkwardly readjusting on his arm. Zidane is thus indicating in spite of himself that he wants to leave the pitch and get back to the changing rooms. He no longer has the means, or the strength, the energy, the will to effect one last masterstroke, one last gesture of pure form – the header, so exquisite, stopped by Buffon a few moments earlier will open his eyes once and for all to his incurable impotence. The form, right now, resists him – and it is unacceptable for an artist, we are familiar with the intimate bonds that unite art and melancholy. Incapable of scoring a goal, he will mark minds.

Night has fallen over Berlin now, the intensity of the light has faded and Zidane has suddenly felt the sky darkening over his shoulders, leaving nothing in the firmament but the flayed trails of black and pink clouds. *Water mixed with night is an old remorse that will not sleep*[V].

No one in the stadium has understood what just happened. From my seat in the stands of the Olympic Stadium I saw the match resuming, the Italians going on the attack once more and the action moving towards the opposite goal. An Italian player was left on the ground, the gesture had taken place, Zidane had been captured by the hostile gods of melancholy. The referee stopped the game, and they started to run in all directions across the pitch, towards the prostrate player and towards the linesman, who was surrounded by Italian players, my gaze moved from left to right, then, through my binoculars, I pinpointed Zidane, instinctively, the eye is always drawn towards Zidane, the outline of Zidane in a white jersey standing in the night in the middle of the pitch, his face in extreme close-up in the sights of my binoculars, and Buffon, the Italian goalkeeper, appearing from nowhere and starting to talk to him and rubbing his head, massaging his skull and the back of his neck, in a surprising gesture, caressing, enfolding, a rubbing gesture that one might use to soothe, to calm a newborn child. I didn't understand what was happening, no one in the stadium understood what was happening, the referee headed towards the little group of players in which Zidane was standing, and took a black card from his pocket, holding it up in the direction of the Berlin sky, and I immediately understood that it was meant for Zidane, the black card of melancholy.

Zidane's gesture, invisible, incomprehensible, is all the more spectacular in that it didn't take place. It quite simply didn't take place, if we stick to direct observation of the events in the stadium, and the legitimate trust that we can place in our senses, no one saw anything, neither the spectators nor the referees. Not only did Zidane's gesture not take place but, even if it had taken place, even if Zidane had had the crazed intention, desire or fantasy to headbutt one of his opponents, Zidane's head should never have hit his adversary because, each time Zidane's head had travelled half of the distance separating him from his adversary's torso, it would still have had another half to travel, then another half, then another half again, and so on for ever, so that Zidane's head, advancing towards its target but never reaching it, as in a vast slow-motion sequence on an eternal loop, will never, ever be able to, it's physically and mathematically impossible (that's Zidane's paradox, if not Zeno's), make contact with the adversary's torso – never, only the fleeting impulse that passed through Zidane's mind was visible to the eyes of television viewers all over the world.

[i] Jean-Philippe Toussaint, *The Bathroom*, (tr. Nancy Amphoux and Paul Angelis).

[ii] Jean-Philippe Toussaint, *The Bathroom*, (tr. Nancy Amphoux and Paul Angelis).

[iii] Jean Starobinski, *L'encre de la mélancholie*.

[iv] Sigmund Freud, *A Childhood Memory of Leonardo da Vinci*.

[v] Gaston Bachelard, *Water and Dreams*, (tr. Edith R. Farrell).

Current and forthcoming books by Fitzcarraldo Editions

2014
Zone by Mathias Enard
Memory Theatre by Simon Critchley

2015
On Immunity by Eula Biss
My Documents by Alejandro Zambra
It's No Good by Kirill Medvedev
Street of Thieves by Mathias Enard
Notes on Suicide by Simon Critchley
Pond by Claire-Louise Bennett
Nicotine by Gregor Hens
Nocilla Dream by Agustín Fernández Mallo

2016
Pretentiousness: Why it Matters by Dan Fox
Counternarratives by John Keene
Second-hand Time by Svetlana Alexievich
The Hatred of Poetry by Ben Lerner
A Primer for Cadavers by Ed Atkins
Bricks and Mortar by Clemens Meyer
The Doll's Alphabet by Camilla Grudova

2017
Nocilla Experience by Agustín Fernández Mallo
This Young Monster by Charlie Fox
Compass by Mathias Enard
Essayism by Brian Dillon

Subscribe to Fitzcarraldo Editions:
fitzcarraldoeditions.com/subscribe

Fitzcarraldo Editions
243 Knightsbridge
London, SW7 1DN
United Kingdom

ISBN 978-1-910695-17-3

Design by Ray O'Meara
Typeset in Fitzcarraldo
Printed and bound by TJ International

Fitzcarraldo Editions